A TEENAGER WHO DARED TO OBEY GOD

Leona Sumrall Murphy

PUBLICATION

P.O. Box 12
South Bend, IN 46624

Unless otherwise indicated,
all Scripture quotations are taken from
the *King James Version* of the Bible.

A Teenager Who Dared To Obey God
ISBN O-937580-39-2
Copyright © 1985 by Lester Sumrall
Evangelistic Association
Published by LeSEA Publishing Company
P.O. Box 12
South Bend, Indiana 46624

Printed in the United States of America.
All rights reserved under international
Copyright Law. Contents and/or cover may
not be reproduced in whole or in part in any
form without the express written consent of
the Publisher.

CONTENTS

Foreword

On December 29, 1983, my wife Frances and I sat in a restaurant across the table from Dr. Lester Sumrall, along with his sister, Leona Sumrall Murphy, and her husband, the Reverend James Murphy.

Although Dr. Sumrall and I have visited together a number of times over the years, it had been some twenty-five years since I had seen Brother and Sister Murphy. Seeing them brought so many emotions to surface for this preacher as I remembered the story that my family had related to me so many, many times. I reached across the table and took Sister Murphy's hand in mine and related to her that story—a story for which I shall never cease to thank and praise God.

In 1936 Sister Leona came with her mother to our little hometown of Ferriday, Louisiana, to bring the Gospel message of Jesus Christ. She was only a girl, 17 or 18 years old. God had spoken to the two of them and told them that they should build a church in that city. So they proceeded to find a lot. When they had located one, they went out and began pulling weeds with their bare hands to clear the ground for the church God had told them to build. They had nothing to work with and no money to hire the work done, but God had spoken to "Mother" Sumrall and Leona, and they *would* somehow build a church in Ferriday.

Of course, God had everything timed, as *He* always does. Just one year previously (March 15, 1935), I had been born in Ferriday in the home of my uncle, Lee Calhoun. Now Uncle Lee just happened to be one of the wealthiest men in the parish (county)—and he *just happened* to come by that lot on the same lovely spring day that these two beautiful Christian ladies were pulling weeds! He stopped the pickup truck in which he and I were riding and asked the two women what they were doing. Little did he know that his eternal destiny, as well as that of so very many family members, would be charted at this meeting.

To Dr. Lester Sumrall, elder statesman of the great Gospel of Jesus Christ, author, missionary, and evangelist, I say thank you for providing so much of the spiritual foundation that has helped this ministry to be brought to pass.

Sister Leona, forever I thank you and your wonderful mother for the unselfish love and burden that brought you to the little town where we lived. Among the many stories of miracles and victories related in your book, may this simple account of our being brought to Jesus be a blessing to all who read it—even as you have been a blessing to us. I suspect that forever and forever I will shout aloud:

Oh, happy day,
Oh, happy day,
When Jesus washed
My sins away.

Jimmy Swaggart

Dedication

This book is dedicated to the young men and women who have accepted the challenge of performing the sacred task of preaching the Gospel.

Being young is a great experience. You have all your life before you. God gives you a natural appeal that attracts other people to accept the same vision God has given you.

Your unlimited energy, abounding health, and your joy of living for God, will draw the attention of other young people that have nothing but disadvantages, frustration and disappointments in their lives.

In all stages of your life be as Caleb in his remarkable example of FAITH. As a young man he was chosen to be one of the twelve spies sent to spy out the land of Canaan for the people of Israel. According to Numbers, chapter 13, Caleb's faith gave him unusual courage. When they came back, ten spies said, "The people are strong, and the cities are fortified." However, Caleb and Joshua said, "Let us go up at once and possess it. We are well able."

Faith gave Caleb the courage to stand against the majority. Caleb's faith gave him patience. At no time do we see him griping or complaining. He always kept his faith and courage, and we never read that he gave up.

There will be times of unfulfilled dreams and frustrations, but keep your faith and learn to walk without fainting.

In Joshua, chapter 14, when Israel had crossed into the land, Caleb was 85 years old and he came to Joshua and said, "Give me this mountain!" He assured him his body was strong, his spirit was strong, and his faith was even stronger.

In Joshua 15:14, he drove out the three sons of Anak even though they were giants, and they fled.

God still uses specialized individuals who exalt Jehovah above others. The same fire of evangelism that burned in my heart as a teenager is still aflame today.

Let the rest of your life be the best of your life in working for Jesus.

1

GOD'S CALL

I can do all things through Christ which strengtheneth me.

Philippians 4:13

"Go to Ferriday!"

"Was that God, or my imagination?" I asked myself. I was shaking like a leaf. Silently I prayed, "But God, I was asking about St. Joseph, Louisiana."

Mother stopped praying and looked at me.

"Did God speak to you?"

"Yes!"

"Is it Ferriday, Louisiana?"

"Yes!"

God had also spoken to her heart. A surge of joy swept through our souls. Tears began to flow down our faces. We had passed through Ferriday, but we did not know any of the people.

When I hear someone mention Ferriday, Louisiana, I am reminded of three cousins: Jimmy Swaggart, Jerry Lee Lewis, and Mickey Gilley whose names are familiar to almost everyone today. But these three famous cousins were only small boys and known to no one outside of their own circle of family and friends when God called Mother Sumrall and me to go and minister in their hometown of Ferriday.

Of course, we had no idea then that one day they would rise to such heights of international fame. In fact, looking back, that whole mission to Ferriday was an extraordinary move of God with consequences far beyond our limited view.

At that time, Mother and I were staying with relatives in Mobile, Alabama. We were earnestly seeking God's will for our lives, when suddenly Mother had a vision of an open-air meeting with people everywhere. She saw the colorful clothes the people were wearing as they arrived in trucks, buses, and the "touring cars" popular in that day.

A few days later we received a letter from Mother's youngest brother who lived in Waterproof, Louisiana. In the letter he said that he was coming to Mobile the following week and for us to be ready to return home with him. We checked our food supply, and there was only enough food to last us one week. We didn't know (but God knew!) that we would never return to Mobile, Alabama, to live.

When we arrived at my uncle's home he took us into a large room which the family seldom used. He said, "You and Sis feel free to use this room for prayer and Bible reading." It proved to be a blessing, although for a time I questioned why we were in this little Mississippi River town.

One afternoon as I walked into my uncle's place of business, a little girl was making a purchase. My uncle looked up, and seeing me he said casually, "Here comes the lady preacher." When she heard that, the little girl became excited and exclaimed, "The Christians in our prayer group have been praying for God to send us a minister. Our preacher moved to California."

The following Sunday while taking a

drive in the country with my uncle, we saw a man and woman out walking in their garden. We stopped and asked them if they had any fresh eggs for sale. To our surprise, they were the parents of the little girl I had met the week before. We visited together for a while, and they seemed interested in knowing all about us, and what had brought us to their city.

The following week two men came and invited us to preach in their home prayer meeting on Saturday night and Sunday afternoon. When we got there we saw that they had a large living room and that it was full of people. New arrivals kept coming until every available place was taken.

Everything went well on Saturday night. Sunday afternoon after I had preached we invited the people to kneel for prayer. As we were praying a small baby crawled into the kitchen and found an open can of lye. In a few minutes we heard a loud scream. The mother ran into the kitchen and soon returned with the baby. His lips were swollen and he was spitting skin and blood out of his mouth. We prayed and the baby went to sleep. When he woke up the swelling was gone, and the baby was able to nurse. Those attending the meeting marveled at how quickly the Lord had healed the child. This incident gave the people faith in our ministry.

When summer came, the people of that prayer group asked if we could build a brush arbor and hold a revival. They cut down young trees and trimmed them for poles, standing them up in the ground. They then took smaller poles and made a lattice of them across the top on which they laid branches to form a roof. Blocks of wood with planks of lumber on top of them served as crude benches. In the evening meetings light was provided by gasoline lanterns hung on posts.

We announced the services and crowds came from all over that part of the country. People brought their whole families with them. The first Sunday afternoon, the brush arbor was full of people. Those outside stood as near as possible so they could hear the preaching of the Word.

From the first service God gave us many converts. After a week of meetings I decided that the people would be happy to provide a love offering. I borrowed a man's hat to use as an offering plate. I passed it around, but when it came back it had one nickel in it! One solitary five-cent piece for a week's hard work! Was I discouraged? I should say NOT, a thousand times no!! Money was not my motive for being there. I had a burning desire to bring people to the knowledge of the Lord Jesus Christ. I LOVED to preach.

One night as I was preaching, I noticed a commotion outside the brush arbor. I didn't pay much attention and went right on with my sermon. Later I found out that some of the boys had brought a goat and were planning to wait until I reached the climax of my message, then as the altar call was given for sinners to come forward for salvation, one of the boys was going to ride the goat down the center aisle and break up the meeting.

There was a man present who, along with his family, never missed a service. Their mode of transportation was an old flat-bed truck. The man would never get out of the cab of the truck, but the wife and children would come into the meeting. We were told that he was a man of few words, and was supposed to have killed several men. The man saw the goat and heard the boys laughing. Walking over to where they were standing, he asked the boys what they were doing. They told him how they were planning to ride the goat down the aisle and "bust up the meeting." The man looked at them coldly and calmly replied, "If you do, I'll shoot the goat out from under the one that rides him, and then I'll shoot the boy." Knowing the man and his reputation, that quickly put a damper on the boys' fun.

When the meeting was over, the man told his wife to invite Mother and me over for the noon meal the following day. This was a surprise to his wife because he had never before invited any preacher to his home. We agreed to go and upon our arrival we found a simple home. It was clean and the wife had cooked a delicious meal. While sitting at the table the man related the incident about the goat. Placing his pistol by his plate, he laid his hand on it and said, "This gun has been my friend for a long time. It was your friend last night. Believe me, I would have shot any boy who tried to disturb that meeting." We believed him!

The revival continued most of the summer. While we were there, we were invited to serve as pastors of a church in St. Joseph, Louisiana, a small town a few miles north. We prayed for several days but the Spirit of the Lord did not seem to be leading us to accept the church.

Ferriday is a small-size delta town located about eighty miles southeast of Monroe, Louisiana, and eighty-five miles northwest of the capital city of Baton Rouge. We were told that it was a wicked town and that it was a regular event there for someone to be stabbed or shot. We were warned that it was dangerous to drive through the town after dark. The more we prayed, the more certain we were that God was leading us to Ferriday. The joy we felt made us know we had made the right decision, and we were happy to make a total dedication to obey God's call.

Then God spoke to us through prophecy by the Holy Spirit:

"I have valuable treasures in this town. They are hidden from the view of man. These jewels will be carefully shaped by My Spirit. Their dedication will surpass those around them. To salvage this treasure you must dig with caution. Your patience will be tried, but I will bring them forth as pure gold. Your lives will display My love and I will draw them to Myself. They will see that your dedication is not shallow and will seek to pattern their lives according to your Christian living.''

I told my uncle that God had told us to go to Ferriday.

"When do you want to go?" he asked.

"We're ready to go now!"

In less than an hour we were on our way.

When we arrived in Ferriday I decided to start at the top. I went to call on Mr. Volgt who was the city mayor and owned the only drugstore in town. When I walked into his office I was bubbling over. I was so full of enthusiasm I could hardly contain myself.

I told Mr. Volgt who we were and that, as Mother and I had been praying, God had laid Ferriday upon our hearts. I asked him to grant us a permit to hold a youth revival in the city.

To our pleasant surprise he said that he would not only give us a permit to hold the revival, but that he wanted to have a part in it. He took out his pen and wrote a substantial check to help us financially.

Leaving the mayor's office, we began to look for a vacant lot on which to hold the open-air meeting. A large open plot was found, bordering on what was then the main highway passing through town. We inquired as to who owned the property and were told that a Mr. Corbett was the owner and that he could be found at his sawmill which was located near the edge of town.

A friend offered to drive us out to see Mr. Corbett. As we were driving onto the parking lot, it started raining. Mother and I rushed inside. The rain soon became a downpour. (It seemed to rain longer and harder in Louisiana than any place we had ever known.)

The secretary asked us the nature of our business. I was still bursting with enthusiasm. I began to tell her of our visit to see my uncle and that while Mother and I were there praying, God had told us to come to Ferriday to hold an open-air revival. I continued to tell her what God could and would do.

The secretary, with a sober look on her face, replied, "But you are so young."

"Yes, that's why God has called me," I said brightly. "I will attract the youth. God wants to change this town!"

The rain was coming down in torrents by this time. The secretary reached for her raincoat and hat, took an umbrella from the stand and said, "I'll be right back." She approached a car in which a man and a woman were sitting, involved in a deep conversation. After the secretary had talked to the man for a few moments, the car door opened, the man reached for the umbrella and ran toward the office. Shaking the water off the umbrella, he placed it back in the stand in the corner. He invited us into his office and after we were seated he asked, "What is it you want to do for the youth of this town?"

I repeated my story. He was very interested and said, "The lot is yours."

"For how long?" I asked.

"For as long as you need it."

"Well, I will need a paper with your signature on it saying that I have the lot for an indefinite period of time," I told him. "I want to stay here long enough to do a good job and not have to move on before God's work has been accomplished."

Mr. Corbett had his secretary type up the agreement. Then he added his signature to the bottom of the page and handed the document to me.

Much preparation was needed before the revival could begin. I belonged to a church organization at that time, so I decided to contact the superintendent and share with him my burden for Ferriday. At first he was not too excited, but asked what we wanted him to do. I told him that we needed some plank seats and a platform. He smiled and said, "I don't have a lumber mill."

I said, "I know a man who does."

"O.K. If you can get the lumber for the seats and platform," he agreed, "then I'll send some men down to do the work."

The men came, but had to return before the platform was completed. When they came back, they brought a large red, white, and blue sign announcing the date and hour of the revival. The ladies of the church bought a secondhand paino and the men brought it down with them.

Mother and I rented a two-bedroom apartment and the superintendent promised that his congregation would donate groceries. He also said that he had several

Bible school students in his home for the summer who would like a place to minister. His daughter, Mary, could play the piano for us, and Beulah Vale, who was a preacher, could help me minister the Word. We were happy to have the two young ladies join our efforts.

We had no transportation so we had to walk every place we went. As we walked up and down the streets we knew we were being observed by the town folk. We heard that we were referred to as "the two ladies in white." There were many questions concerning our being there. Who were we? Where had we come from? Why were we there? All this time, preparation was being made for the outdoor meeting.

2

OPEN-AIR MEETING

*Again, the kingdom of heaven is like
unto a net, that was cast into the sea, and
gathered of every kind.*

Matthew 13:47

Never will I forget the thrill of the
first night of the meeting in Ferriday!
Before leaving the apartment, I raised my
hands to God and asked Him to stand by
me. When we walked on the grounds, the
seats were filled and the people were still
coming. Cars were parked everywhere.

Mary Turner and Beulah Vale were
playing the piano and singing. Their
voices were like those of angels. From
their hearts rolled forth the beautiful
hymns of the church.

A young couple returning home from vacation saw the large crowd and stopped. They stood near the edge, their faces shining with enthusiasm and expectancy. The preaching with Holy Ghost anointing was already in progress. The Spirit and the presence of God began to move over the audience. After speaking for almost an hour, I asked the people to bow their heads while I prayed. When I finished the prayer for the unsaved, I asked them to stand and come forward. The people came from all directions!

The young couple returning from vacation seemed moved, and the husband, Henry Herron, came to the front and accepted Jesus as his Savior. He was my first convert. From that night on, he and his family attended the meetings.

I invited the people to open their Bible to Revelation 21:8, and began reading the text, *But the fearful, and unbelieving, and the abominable, and murderers, and whoremongers, and sorcerers, and idolaters, and all liars, shall have their part in the lake which burneth with fire and brimstone: which is the second death.*

The audience burst into laughter. I could not imagine what was so funny.

After the meeting they explained that I forgot to say that in Ferriday they are fearful, unbelieving, abominable, and murderers.

In this outdoor meeting we dealt with drunkards, gamblers, prostitutes, bootleggers, liars, and thieves. You name it, every sin one could imagine seemed to be represented. The horrible sins some of those people confessed would almost make one's hair stand on end!

I wondered how some of those people had managed to stay out of prison. I never knew until I went to Ferriday that the devil could be so mean to people. A father was in prison for bootlegging whiskey when his little son died. Two officers brought him home in chains to attend the funeral. As soon as the funeral was over, the father was put into the patrol car and returned to prison. Both the mother and father were in tears as the patrol car rolled away.

There are many sad stories of crime and death I could relate. It was common to hear of federal agents raiding an illegal whiskey still and arresting the men and sending them off to prison. Our neighbor, while working at an illegal still, was scalded.

There was an explosion and his flesh was literally cooked on his body. He died a few hours later. We visited the home of his heartbroken wife and daughter and prayed for God to comfort their hearts. The lady could not understand why her husband had to be killed when he was only trying to supply food for his family.

The Gospel also attracted many beautiful, law-abiding men and women that lived a good moral life. As the Word of God was preached, the Holy Spirit dealt with these people and they, too, became dedicated born-again Christians.

The devil was mad. Up to this time only a few of the people had made an effort to get acquainted with us. The meeting had been in progress for more than a week when Satan sent a mob to try to frighten us away. When I went to the platform to open the service with prayer, I noticed some men standing in a circle on the edge of the lot. They talked constantly. Beulah was the speaker and she did not seem disturbed by their continual mumbling. After she finished her sermon and gave the altar call, several came forward.

Unknown to us, Mary and Beulah

were approached by the men after the meeting. I wondered why the two girls rushed off to the apartment, leaving us to walk alone. Several people were visiting with friends, so we waited until everyone was gone before turning out the lights.

There was a path that led to the road with high weeds on both sides. When Mother and I were ready to leave, I noticed a group of men were standing in the center of the path. I thought this was strange and when I looked around I noticed that not one person was left except Mother and I.

When God told us to go to Ferriday He told us not be afraid of their faces. So I felt that if I didn't have to be afraid of their faces, I didn't have to be afraid of the men. When I started walking down that path I had no fear of men or devils. I did not slow up, but walked the same pace I always walked. When I reached this group, they stepped out into the weeds. I said, "Good night!" A man with a deep voice quietly said, "Good night."

When we reached the apartment the two girls were standing outside waiting for us. They were fearful the men would try to harm us. They had threatened the two girls saying that if we four women didn't get out of town somebody was going to die. The men advised them we were not to conduct one more meeting in Ferriday.

Beulah said she pointed to me and said, "The youngest lady is in charge." She did not know why she made the statement, but she said, "That lady is as strong as iron and if I know her, she will be here tomorrow night." She was right. I was there! If any of the mob returned, they did not make themselves known.

On another night I asked someone in the audience to tell of a healing they had received. When they sat down, a man whom I had never seen before stepped onto the platform and began to talk. I sat there for a few moments. God spoke to my heart and said, "This is a very sinful man." I walked up behind him and in a low voice said, "Go sit down!" He stopped that moment, returned to his seat and sat by a young girl holding a baby.

The next day I was walking out of the post office when one of the businessmen stopped and said, "I visited the meeting last night. Did you know the man who stepped to the platform and tried to take over?" I said, "No, I have never seen him before." "Do you mind telling me what you said to him?" I looked into the face of the businessman and said, "Sir, the Lord told me that he is a very sinful man and to tell him to sit down. So I obeyed the Lord." He continued, "The young lady he sat with in the audience is his daughter. It is a case of incest. He is the father of the child she was holding. The people in Ferriday have watched you and your mother. We know that you are Christians and appreciate what you are doing."

One Saturday we were standing in the yard when one of our young converts drove up and introduced us to his friend. He said the man was a preacher and asked if he could preach for us on Sunday. I felt a check in my spirit. I tried to be kind and told him we could not use him at this time. After talking for fifteen minutes the young convert began to be persistent and urged me to let him preach. He said he was visiting relatives who lived next door and they wanted to hear him preach.

The spirit of prophecy came upon me and I began to prophesy, "This man is not a preacher. He has committed a serious crime. An officer of the law will soon be here looking for him."

The so-called preacher became nervous and urged the new convert to leave. After they were gone Mother said, "I wonder what this means? I have never heard you speak in this manner before." The following Monday an officer of the law knocked on the door inquiring about this man.

I said, "Sir, you may not believe that God talks to people. God warns His children concerning wicked people." I told him the story of how the spirit of prophecy spoke through me saying this man had committed a crime and that an officer of the law would soon be here looking for him. I asked, "Has this man committed a terrible crime?" The policeman was shocked. It was hard for him to believe what he was hearing. He turned pale, his hands began to shake and he said, "Yes, he has." As he left, he stumbled several times returning to his car.

Night after night the homemade benches were filled. As far as one could see cars were parked on either side of the road. The audience was attentive to the preaching of God's Word.

A tall thin man with snow-white hair was attracted to the meetings and never missed a night. We could see he was interested in what was happening. He tried to participate in every way. When we prayed, he knelt and prayed. When we passed the offering plate, he always gave. When we sang, he would try to sing along with us. I described him to our landlady, telling her of his faithful attendance each night. She said, "I know who you are talking about; that is Lee Calhoun. He is a millionaire many times over. He is popular with the politicians. When there is an election, the politician he promotes always wins. He never loses. The man he supports is always elected, from the governor's office right down to the local sheriff."

She painted a pretty bad picture of the man. As far as I knew, she never attended a meeting, but Lee Calhoun would come and enjoy the preaching of the Word and even showed signs of wanting to accept Christ.

One morning the landlady knocked on my door and said, "The Methodist church has a tent revival each summer. I attended the meeting last night. The minister opened the doors of the church for those who wanted to become members. Lee Calhoun's wife joined. The minister asked Lee to become a member along with his wife. He told the minister, 'No! When I join a church, I will join a church just like the two ladies have down on the open lot.' He was speaking of you and your mother.''

One Sunday afternoon, Mr. Calhoun came to our door and invited us to his house for the evening meal. He said that usually their cook was off on Sunday, but he had asked her to work so she could cook us a good chicken dinner. I feel sure that we were the first preachers ever invited to his home. We had been there only a few minutes when the Calhouns began to ask us questions about the Bible. We answered them as best we could until it was time to go to church. Although Mr. Calhoun was not well-educated, he was a successful businessman. Despite his rough exterior, he was kind and open to the Gospel.

3

ELMO JR.

And these words, which I command thee this day, shall be in thine heart: And thou shalt teach them diligently unto thy children...
                    Deuteronomy 6:6-7

One day Henry came to the apartment to ask if we would go and pray with his sister Mamie who had lost her son. We went with him and found a broken-hearted, grief-stricken mother. As it turned out, Mamie was Mrs. Elmo Lewis, the mother of two sons, Elmo Jr. and Jerry Lee, who was later to become a well-known rock-n-roll singer. When we entered the house, Mrs. Lewis was holding in her hand a little sock she had found behind the trunk. The sock belonged to Elmo Jr., who had been killed in an accident a few days before.

We had heard that a little boy had jumped off a wagon into the path of a car and lost his life. We didn't know, however, that the little boy's mother was the sister of Henry Herron, the young man who had been converted the first night of the revival meeting.

Mrs. Lewis was so shaken it was all she could do to control her emotions long enough to tell us about her son. She said that Elmo Jr. had been very interested in the open-air meetings, and had attended almost every night. Each morning he would discuss the message which had been preached the night before. He would ask his mother questions, many of which she was unable to answer.

One morning, with a very inquiring look upon his face, the little boy began asking his mother one question after another.

"Who is God?"

"He is our Creator."

"Do you know God?"

"I don't think so ..."

"Why not?"

"I don't know..."

"Where does God live?"

"Up in heaven..."

"Can I go to heaven?"

"Maybe..."

Mrs. Lewis said that she was shocked at his interest and persistence. She tried to explain to him the best she knew how, but without much success. She said she realized how ignorant she was when it came to the Bible.

He kept attending the meetings, she told us, and continued to ask her questions about God. One day she was tired and nervous and told him to go into the yard and play, they would talk about it later. It was then that he walked to the corner and hopped on the back of a wagon. When he jumped off he was in the path of an oncoming car and was killed instantly. The shock and grief were almost more than she could bear. She was tortured by her loss and tormented by remorse and self-condemnation because she had not been able to teach her son about God.

We prayed with her and felt that God gave her a measure of comfort. After that, she and her two sisters began attending the meetings and singing in the choir.

Elmo, Sr., Jerry Lee's father, was a tall man with dark eyes and black hair. I never saw him without a big smile on his face. One day he came to the parsonage. He sat down, crossed his legs, and said, "Sister Sumrall, I am just a farm boy. I don't have a good education, and I don't know anything about the Bible, but I do want to go to heaven when I die. I like what you preach. You say we must live above sin. I don't think anyone in Ferriday can live above sin besides you and Mother Sumrall." I explained that God loved him and gave His Son Jesus that all who call upon His name would be saved. "You say you can't live for God. I know you can't, not on your own, but Christ will live it through you." Looking straight into his face I said, "Elmo, God will give you strength to live for Him one day at a time until Jesus calls you home." With tears in his eyes he said, "You and Mother Sumrall love us and you have tried so hard to get us saved." I assured him that we loved him and his family very much and we offered to pray for him, but he did not accept Christ. When he left, all three of us were weeping.

4

A VACANT LOT
BECOMES A CHURCH

> *...the true tabernacle, which the Lord
> pitched and not man.*
> *Hebrews 8:2*

The open-air revival continued all
summer. Then the rainy season set in but
the people continued to come. In one
hand they held an umbrella and in the
other a Bible. I am sure it looked strange
to those passing by to see the people sitting in the rain while I preached. It was
time for Mary and Beulah to return to
Bible school.

Mother and I felt that the Lord
would have us build a church. We went to
see Mr. Corbett, the businessman who

had loaned us the lot for the revival. When we asked about a lot on which to build a church, he took us in his car around town to look at several possible locations. We picked a large lot on Texas Avenue. The following night we announced to the audience that we would be building a church. I said, "We do not have the money to build a church, but God will provide."

One day as Mr. Calhoun was driving through Ferriday, he turned onto Texas Avenue and saw Mother and me out on the vacant lot. He stopped his truck and asked what we were doing. I said, "We are getting the land ready to build a church."

The weeds were almost as tall as we were. We told him that a man had promised to come out and cut the weeds but did not show up. When Mr. Calhoun saw the blisters on our hands he said, "The weeds will be cut, you two go on home. Are you sure you are going to build a church there?"

Mother replied very pleasantly, "Yes, we are."

Mr. Calhoun asked, "Who is financing this project?"

"God is," Mother answered. "The Lord sent us here and we are doing this in obedience to Him."

Mr. Calhoun said, "God? You mean God actually spoke to you?"

Mother answered, "That's right! He sure did."

Mr. Calhoun walked back to his truck, shaking his head in disbelief. He had never heard anyone talk this way. How could two women say that God had spoken to them? Jimmy remembered he was in the truck with his uncle this particular day.

It was my habit to get up before daybreak to read the Bible and pray. The kitchen table was the only private place I could find. We had a homemade table but we did not have a tablecloth, so over the table we had spread a bedsheet that reached to the floor. I would crawl under the table to shut myself in with God. I would often pray for two or three hours at a time. The table faced the main entrance to the apartment, so I could not get out from under the kitchen table without being seen from the front door. Suddenly there came a knock on the door. I said to myself, "If I answer, the person at the door will see me crawl out of here and think I am crazy." So I waited. I heard a man clear his throat and continue to knock. Finally I decided to make a move.

The person at the door was Mr. Calhoun, and sure enough he was shocked when he saw me crawling out from under the kitchen table like a kid caught playing hide-and-seek.

"My God a'mighty, woman!" He let slip in his surprise. "What are you doing under the table?"

I explained to him that it was the only private place I had to pray.

I invited him in. As soon as he was seated, he said that he had never worked with a religious group before, but he wanted to help us with the church project.

"How do you go about building a church?" he asked.

I told him that we would visit the local businessmen and ask for donations. He thought that was a good idea so he volunteered to go with me.

When we would come to a tavern or a night club, Mr. Calhoun would suggest that I stand outside while he went in to ask the owner and his customers for a donation.

He, being a rich man, met with opposition from some of the businessmen. They would laugh and ask why he didn't build the church himself, he had enough money. He could not take their jokes and insults. He had never expected any opposition. He had thought the men of the town would appreciate his interest in helping two ladies take donations and would be willing to contribute to the building fund. When he returned home after that first outing, he told us that he would not be going with us anymore to ask for donations.

When he got back home, he was noticeably upset. His wife asked him what was wrong, and he told her that he would not ask the people of that town for donations again, "if those ladies *never* get a church building!" adding, "I am finished!"

When his wife got out of bed the following morning, she was surprised to see Mr. Calhoun still in bed. Normally he was an early riser and would be out of the house before she even woke up. He told her he didn't get up because he couldn't move his legs. She asked him what had happened, and he said he must have had a stroke. She asked him if he wanted Mother and Sister Sumrall to come pray for his legs and he said no, he would be okay.

After an hour or so his wife asked him again if he wanted to send for the lady preachers. He became angry and told her NO, he didn't want anyone to tell those two women about his legs! His wife called a doctor and told him about the situation. He promised to come by and check on Mr. Calhoun the following morning.

The next day we had just finished breakfast when there came a knock at the door and I was told that Mr. Calhoun wanted us to come pray for him. As we walked into the bedroom, I smiled and said, "You know God is expecting you to help build that church."

With a look of guilt on his face, Mr. Calhoun answered, "Yes, I know!"

I prayed for him and that very moment his legs were healed. Everyone in the room was rejoicing. I looked around and the doctor was standing in the doorway almost in shock.

After that, we all got back to work building the church. We hired a finished carpenter to manage the job. He worked ten hours a day, six days a week. We paid him twenty-five dollars a week. I had a friend who was a building contractor. I told him we were going to build a church, so he offered to figure out the materials we would need.

Up to this time I had very little knowledge of building materials. I didn't know a 2x4 from an 8x10 glossy! But I caught on fast. Three different lumber companies donated most of the lumber. When I asked for a donation I always knew exactly what I wanted and the amount we needed. One sawmill owner was asked to donate all the siding and hardwood flooring. When I asked him for the material, he laughed and asked if I wanted him to jump out the window too. But I was not easily put off. We kept talking and he ended up agreeing to give it all to us, if I could at least give him a check for $15 "for his records." To his surprise, I brought a truck to haul the lumber back to the building site. When the church was finished, we had enough siding left over to build a parsonage.

A man I had never met before sent word he wanted to donate bricks for the foundation if we could pick them up. A black brother used his horse and wagon to bring them to the church lot.

Whenever I heard of a man in town who was unemployed, I would go to his home and ask if he would be willing to volunteer a few days' labor, or more, on the church building. Most of the men I approached were willing; some worked one day, while others continued to help until the building was completed.

One day a group of men were laying down roofing material and Mr. Calhoun decided he would help. He would place a sheet of material, then yell, "Nail it!" He could be heard a block away. Then, at the top of his voice, he would begin to sing, "I know the Lord will make a way for me! I know the Lord will make a way for me! If I live a holy life, shun the wrong and do the right, I know the Lord will make a way for me!" By the time he had finished his chorus he would have another sheet in place and would yell out, "Nail it!" By the end of the day the roof was finished.

After the building was completed, we were sitting in a swing on the front porch of Mr. Calhoun's house when Mr. Yancey, a local lumber dealer, came looking for me. He had a bill for the material I had purchased while building the church. I just sat there and agreed that the debt should be paid. After a period of time Mr. Calhoun asked if he could speak with me in his office. When we were alone, he asked me, "Do you have the money to pay this lumber bill?"

"No," I confessed, "I don't have a dime."

"What is the amount you owe?"

"$26," I told him. Then, opening his safe, he said, "I am going to give you the money to pay the bill. If you ever get it, pay it back. If you don't, forget it."

I FORGOT IT!

Only eternity will reveal all that was accomplished for God, and the lives that were changed forever in that "house which the Lord built."

Frame of the Church

Leona in front of parsonage before it was finished.

Mother Sumrall after parsonage was finished.

The little white frame church in Ferriday, Louisiana.

Our first Sunday School staff.

Lee and Stella Calhoun

Mother Sumrall, Beulah, Mary and Leona Sumrall
in an open-air meeting.

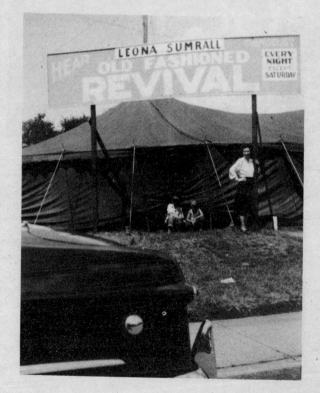

Mother Sumrall and Leona

Mother Sumrall

Leona Sumrall

5

GANGSTERS

*The wicked shall be turned into hell,
and all the nations that forget God.*
                                        Psalm 9:17

One day during the construction of
the church building, I was out walking in
the yard looking at the progress we were
making. As I surveyed our handiwork, I
was approached by a man who was a
stranger to me.

"I am a sign painter," he said. "I
would like to put up a sign in front of the
church."

I told him that I didn't have any
money to pay for a sign.

"Oh, you won't have to pay for it,"
he added. "It will be a donation." He

gathered up some scrap lumber and left. Soon he returned with a beautiful sign.

The man said he had some friends who were carpenters and would be glad to help on the church building. I told him that the outside was about finished, but that two men would be there that night putting in the ceiling. He returned and brought three other men with him. They worked hard and returned each night, except the nights we had services. When the church was finished, we built a small parsonage, and again the four men came to help, but only at night. We never saw them in the daytime.

To the night workers we served hot chocolate and cookies. Each night a different man put money on the table and said it was to pay for the treats for the following night.

At the completion of the construction, the four men disappeared as mysteriously as they had appeared. Several months later there was a knock at our door. It was beginning to get dark. When I answered the door, a well-dressed man said, "Do you remember me?" "Yes, but this is the first time I have seen you dressed up."

"I don't have much time to talk," he said, "so listen very carefully. Do you remember when you were building the church, I offered to build a sign?"

I nodded my head silently.

"Well, I was picking up lumber that day," he went on, "when Mr. Calhoun walked up. When I saw him, I left immediately because I knew him and didn't want him to recognize me. I had bought barrels of bootleg whiskey from him. He also knew that I had killed my wife and baby and thrown their bodies down into an open well. At the time we four men were here working on the church, all of us were hiding out from the law. That's why we could only work at night.

"You two ladies are good women, and I appreciate your letting us come down here for a little outing. We needed to get out of our hideout and get some exercise and fresh air."

Then looking back over his shoulder to make sure no one was listening, he added quietly, "The man we called Blackie was a bank robber. He has been caught and sent to prison. Joe robbed a store and killed the owner. He was arrested a few days ago. Jack has done everything in the book—rape, murder, robbery, you name it. He has not been caught! The guy I'm with now is in trouble, too; he's driving a stolen car."

By this time it was dark. The man in the car ran up to the door and told my visitor it was time to go.

"You said you would only be here a couple of minutes," he said nervously. "Come on, we've got to get out of here!"

The man looked at me. Just before turning to leave, he said, "My last word is, if you don't believe my story, ask Mr. Calhoun if he ever knew a man by the name of J.H. Thank you for trusting us. We didn't deserve it." Then he was gone.

After the two men had left, Mother and I talked about the strange twilight encounter. When I related to her what the man had said, she and I could hardly believe that we had entertained four criminals without ever knowing it. We were glad it was church night because we were anxious to talk to Mr. Calhoun.

That evening I watched for Mr. Calhoun to arrive. As soon as I saw him come in and take a seat, I rushed over and asked him if he had ever known a man near St. Joseph, Louisiana, named J.H.

He replied, "Yes, the last I heard, the law was looking for him. I heard he killed his wife and child and threw their bodies down a well. I have no idea how much whiskey I sold that man. I imagine he was drunk when he committed the crime."

Then, realizing what he was saying, Mr. Calhoun looked at me intently and explained, "You see, I never told you and your mother, but I used to be involved in some pretty shady dealings. When I was younger I used to sell bootleg whiskey. I had several close calls with the law. On one run I was stopped by revenue agents and just missed being caught with a loaded pistol in my truck. But I threw it out the window into the grass where they couldn't see it. It was a wonder I wasn't arrested then. Later on, I was finally caught and convicted of whiskey running and served a one-year prison term."

I didn't tell Mr. Calhoun that the Lord had sent four gangsters, one a former customer of his, to help build the church we were sitting in that night. We had thought these men were local people.

Although it is not scriptural, it seems sometimes God does "work in mysterious ways, His wonders to perform."

6

THE SWAGGART FAMILY

How then shall they call on him in whom they have not believed? and how shall they believe in him of whom they have not heard? and how shall they hear without a preacher?

Romans 10:14

Jimmy Swaggart's father heard the stirring music at the services and decided to join in and play the fiddle. It was his first time in a church service. The entire Swaggart family was very musically inclined and tremendously talented. Jimmy's mother and two aunts were good singers. His mother later said that before attending the Ferriday meetings she had been in church only three times in her whole life, all three times being funerals she had attended as a child. Neither Mr. or Mrs. Swaggart knew anything about God. They didn't even own a Bible. Still, there was something that drew them to the meetings.

Night after night as they sat through the service, the Spirit of the Lord would deal with them. Mr. Swaggart was deeply troubled about accepting Jesus as his Savior. Finally, he couldn't stand the conviction any longer and decided to run away. He thought it would leave if he moved, so he loaded up the truck and left for Rio Hondo, Texas, eight hundred miles away, in the heart of the Rio Grande Valley.

There Jimmy's mother, father, and baby brother, Donnie, all came down with acute pneumonia. Being the youngest, Donnie was the most susceptible, and showed the weakest resistance to the disease which, in those days, often proved fatal.

Since our parsonage was only two blocks from the home of Jimmy's grandparents, they sent for Mother and me to come and pray that God would heal Donnie. When we arrived, the room was full of Swaggart relatives—uncles, aunts, cousins, etc. They were all drunk, waiting for a "death message" from Texas. One of the aunts was so drunk she had to hold onto the furniture to walk.

We prayed for the boy and then returned to the parsonage. Although I wanted to believe that the boy would be healed, after being around the family I just couldn't muster much hope for his recovery because there was absolutely no faith in that home for God to honor. As far as I could tell, none of them were at all interested in putting their trust in the Lord or serving Him.

As I suspected, the following day the family in Ferriday received a message from Texas that little Donnie had died. It was only by the grace of God that Mr. and Mrs. Swaggart were spared. As soon as they were able to travel, they returned to Ferriday.

After their return, Jimmy's father invited us to their home for a meal. We sat at the Swaggart table enjoying a delicious chicken dinner. Jimmy was sitting next to me. About all that I noticed about him then was that he was barefoot and very hungry. There was not a thing about him that would make me think he was anything other than a normal, healthy, growing boy. He looked and acted like any other kid of his age, full of life and energy, and wanting to leave the table before we had finished eating.

Jimmy's father asked him to settle down. But he told his father that he had promised to meet his cousin, Jerry Lee, and they were going to the movies. His father asked Jimmy several questions before giving him permission to go. He reached in his pocket and gave him some coins. With that, Jimmy dashed out the door, slamming it so hard you would have thought it was coming off the hinges.

Jimmy and Jerry Lee were almost like twins; they were inseparable. If you saw Jimmy, Jerry Lee would be nearby, and vice versa. Each Sunday they would attend Sunday School with their parents. If someone had told me then that those two barefoot, tousle-haired youngsters in overalls would one day grow up to become famous and gain the applause and adulation of millions of people, it would have been hard for me to believe.

I have no idea the number of meals I enjoyed with their folks. At Thanksgiving and Christmas we were always invited to one or the other of their homes.

I will never forget the night Jimmy's father came to the Lord. Kneeling at the left side of the altar, tears streaming down his face, he told God he was sorry for his sins. He literally sobbed and agonized before the Lord, asking Him to forgive him of all his sins. God saw his sincerity and gave him a wonderful salvation experience. As he lifted his hands, his face literally shone. I knew he had become a Christian.

Lee Calhoun was sitting on the front seat watching him pray. I was filled with joy. I turned to Mr. Calhoun and said, "Isn't this great!"

I was told later that there had been a misunderstanding between the two men which God healed that night. When Jimmy's father saw Mr. Calhoun, he put his arms around him and there were tears of joy in both men's eyes.

After building the church and serving as pastors of it for several years, Mother and I left Ferriday and went on the evangelistic field. But I was never able to get away from the first burden God gave me for that town. When passing through,

I often stopped and stayed overnight with Irene Gilley or the Calhouns. I was always interested in the growth of the people and the church.

On one occasion we spent the night with Mr. Calhoun and his wife. He asked if I had heard of the strange behavior of Jimmy Swaggart and his cousins.

"What strange things are you talking about?" I asked.

Mr. Calhoun replied, "They call it the gift of prophecy and interpretation of tongues. Jimmy is saying that God has given him a vision. He says God revealed to him that He is going to send a powerful bomb that will destroy entire cities. He claims that in the vision he could hear people screaming as the buildings crumbled. The boys go into the woods behind their house and pray so loud you can hear them for blocks. They stay for hours, saying they are having visions and revelations. I think someone should take a belt and go down there and give those boys a good licking!"

"No," I told him, "as long as a person is praying, that is a good sign. It could be that God is sending a warning through these young boys that destruction is coming upon this world, and it may be nearer than we might think.''

For several years I was busy evangelizing and making trips to the mission field. Jimmy's father became a minister and moved to Wisner, Louisiana, where he built a church and served as its pastor. By this time Jimmy was in high school and many young people were saved and filled with the Holy Spirit through his efforts. His father contacted us to come to Louisiana and hold a revival. Each morning we met in the church to pray for the meetings. The principal of the local high school allowed those who wanted to pray to come and join the prayer group for one hour.

During this time, we would have long talks with Jimmy. He would say, ''I know God has had His hand upon my life since I was nine years old. God revealed to me that I will minister in large auditoriums to thousands of people.'' There was no doubt in my mind that God was going to be a great force in the life of Jimmy Swaggart. I had no idea to what extent God was going to use him, but we encouraged him to move through any door God opened for him.

For several years we lost contact with Jimmy. Then one night we heard him relate his life story. We had not known about the years of ministering in small churches or the financial hardships he and his family had undergone. He told of his time of testing when he proved to God that his dedication to remain a minister of the Gospel was strong and solid.

Jimmy said that while ministering in a small church in the South, he was approached by his uncle, Elmo Lewis, who came driving up in a big Cadillac. Mr. Lewis asked Jimmy to return with him to Memphis, Tennessee. He said that the man who was promoting his son Jerry Lee and many other rock-n-roll singers had sent for Jimmy. This man had heard about Jimmy's musical talent and wanted to meet him. His uncle Elmo assured Jimmy that if he would go back with him, he would become rich and famous.

Although he was experiencing hardships and lack at the time, Jimmy refused the offer. No doubt he had mixed emotions as he said, "No, I can't go!" But, like Moses of old, Jimmy made a difficult but wise decision, *choosing rather to suffer affliction with the people of God, than to enjoy the pleasures of sin for a season; esteeming the reproach of Christ greater riches than the treasures...for he had respect unto the recompense of the reward* (Heb. 11:25,26). God honored his choice and he went on to become a great evangelist. He also became very successful on radio and television and has developed a worldwide ministry which has reached millions with the Gospel of the Lord Jesus Christ.

Years later Jimmy came to Indianapolis, Indiana, to speak in a large auditorium. He had a successful Christian program on WHMB-TV 40, and my brother Lester wanted to present Jimmy an award for good programming. I was privileged to take part in the presentation.

I walked to the platform and asked Jimmy, "Do you recognize me?" At first he wasn't sure, so I told him I was Leona Sumrall Murphy. He then told the audience that the whole Swaggart family might have gone to hell had not Mother Sumrall and Sister Murphy come to Ferriday. Since then I have wondered if I had not obeyed the leading of the Spirit, would these families have gone to hell? Was I the only one God had chosen, or would God have sent someone else?

It does not take the gift of discernment to see that Jimmy Swaggart has complete trust and faith in the God he proclaims to the millions through his evangelistic efforts. He and his beautiful wife are dedicated servants of the Lord who really believe and live the same Gospel they preach.

I will always be grateful to the Lord for calling me to Ferriday, Louisiana, and for allowing me the great privilege and joy of knowing I had a part in leading the Swaggart family to the Lord.

7

IRENE GILLEY

...behold, now is the accepted time; behold, now is the day of salvation.

                    II Corinthians 6:2

Irene is the mother of Mickey Gilley, owner of "Gilley's" supposedly one of the largest night clubs in the world. Irene is a beautiful Christian friend. When we came to Ferriday, she attended church regularly, but she did not know Jesus Christ as her Savior.

One afternoon Irene's heart was heavy with conviction as she came to the church parsonage. When she arrived, no one was at home. We had gone to Black River to preach a funeral. Mr. Calhoun had taken us in his car, but it took most of the day to make the trip because it was a long way there and back.

The sun was going down when Mr. Calhoun let us out of his car. He was driving down Texas Avenue when he met Irene. She was crying as though her heart would break. Mr. Calhoun stopped his car and asked why she was crying. She said, "I want to get saved, but Mother and Sister Sumrall are gone."

"Go back," he told her. "I just let them out at the parsonage."

When she returned she ran in and fell to her knees, still crying as though her heart would break. I thought someone had been in an accident or had died.

"What's wrong?" I asked hurriedly. "Please answer."

Finally, through her sobs she cried out, "I want to be saved!"

We led her in a prayer of commitment to Jesus Christ and God gave her a beautiful experience of salvation. She jumped to her feet and with tears running down her face she hugged Mother, saying, "He is wonderful!"

God made her an intercessor. She spent many hours in prayer at home and in the church. Her spiritual commitment to the Lord was very precious. When the church would have revival, she would always hold morning prayer meetings in her home. Irene was a happy Christian, never having lost the joy and excitement of that first moment when she came to know the Lord and His marvelous love and grace. She loved to worship Him exuberantly, often giving vent to her emotions and shouting at the top of her voice. I have seen her do a beautiful holy dance unto the Lord.

For many years Irene had a strong influence upon Mickey's life, and I'm sure she still does. She says that Mickey still loves and respects God, and I have no doubt that is true.

8

MOLLIE

Deliver my soul from the sword...
                    Psalm 22:20

Mollie was Mr. Calhoun's cook. She had been serving time in Angola State Prison, but he was able to get her paroled to his custody. Mr. Calhoun owned more rental property than anyone else in town, and Mollie lived in one of his rental houses.

One night she was in a local tavern past the midnight hour when her ex-boyfriend came in and began to curse and threaten. They had quite a heated argument and the boyfriend took a long-blade knife from his pocket. Mollie ran toward the door, but there were two steps she had to go down to get out of the building. Just as she reached the bottom step, the boyfriend reached the steps. He leaped forward and plunged the knife into the back of her head.

She had to walk approximately one mile to her employer's house. Unlocking the door, she walked in, turned on the light, and woke up Mr. Calhoun. When he saw the wound in her head, he jumped out of bed, put on his clothes, and said, "I will take you to the hospital."

"I've already been to the hospital," Mollie said, "but the doctor wouldn't pull the knife out because I didn't have any money."

Mr. Calhoun had a loud voice and he used it to its fullest potential to protest the inhumanity and callousness of the doctor.

"Don't you worry," he assured Mollie. "When I get there, they'll pull it out!"

Mr. Calhoun hurried Mollie out to his car, but it wouldn't start! No other car was available, so the two of them set out walking the ten or twelve blocks to the hospital. When they got there, Mollie sent word to us, "Tell Mother and Sister Sumrall to pray for me and I will make it."

The doctor on duty took Mr. Calhoun aside and explained to him, "Mr. Calhoun, if I pull the knife out of her head, she will die."

Mr. Calhoun exploded, "Well, doctor, she can't live with that knife in her head!"

Mr. Calhoun went in and told Mollie what the doctor had said, that she could live a few hours with the knife in her head, but when it was removed, she would die instantly. Mollie replied, "Mr. Calhoun, tell him to pull it out."

The doctor and the night nurse took a pair of tongs and fastened them to the handle of the knife. They pulled with all the strength they had, but the knife would not budge. Finally, the doctor walked into the waiting room and told Mr. Calhoun that he needed help to pull the knife out. The blade had gone through the roof of Mollie's mouth and blood was running out of it. Both men braced themselves and made several attempts to extract the knife. Finally it came out. When it did, Mollie gave a little sigh of relief. Never during the whole incident did she lose consciousness. In a few days she was released from the hospital.

9

THE BACHELOR

...Today shalt thou be with me in paradise.

Luke 23:43

It was past midnight. We had been asleep several hours when there came a knock at the door. Before I could get my robe on, there was a second knock. I heard a man's voice call my name. When I opened the door, Mr. Calhoun was standing there.

"Would you and Mother Sumrall come with me to the hospital?" he asked. "A man is dying with cancer. The doctor told his family he will not live through the night. He is a bachelor in his late fifties, whom I have known for years. To my knowledge the family never was religious."

Having been informed that her brother would not live through the night, the man's sister had asked Mr. Calhoun if he would find a preacher to come pray for him.

"You and Mother Sumrall are the only preachers in town I know, who really know how to pray," said Mr. Calhoun.

I glanced at the clock; the sick man did not have much time left. Mr. Calhoun offered to drive us to the hospital in his car. When we stepped outside to get into the car, the night seemed so dark. As we entered the hospital no one was stirring. Everything was quiet. We started down the long hallway. At the end of the corridor we saw a dim light. Lifting his hand to point to the door, Mr. Calhoun whispered, "That is Mr. White's room."

We opened the door and I glanced around the room. Several members of the man's family were there. Then I looked at the man on the bed. His stomach was swollen and his voice was weak; I could scarcely hear him when he spoke. I could see that his time was fast running out. This was no time to play games!

I leaned down near his ear and said, "Mr. White, do you know that the doctor has told your family your condition is serious?"

He nodded his head.

"Do you want me to pray for you?"

Very faintly, he answered, "Yes, I do!"

I prayed as I would want someone to pray for me if the doctor had said I had only three hours to live. I asked God to forgive him of all his sins, that without Christ he was going to hell. Tears began to run down his face. After I had finished praying, I told him the story of the crucifixion of Jesus and that He had died for all the sins of the world. Crucified on either side of Jesus were two thieves, I told him. One of the criminals asked Jesus to remember him when He came into His kingdom. In His last minutes Jesus promised the thief that that very day he would be with Him in Paradise.

Then I said to Mr. White, "Jesus will do the same for you."

"I remember that story," he said. "But doesn't the Bible say, 'Believe and *be baptized,* and you will be saved'?"

He looked so sad as he said, "Lady, I'm too sick. I'm not able to be baptized."

"Do you believe in Jesus?" I asked. "Yes."

"Would you be willing to be baptized if you could?"

"Yes."

I said, "We are going to have a simulated baptism."

I laid my hand upon his head and said, "I baptize you in the name of the Father, the Son, and the Holy Ghost." I pushed his head down as far as I could into his pillow. When I released him, I told him to give thanks to Jesus for saving him from all of his sins.

"Now you are ready for heaven," I assured him.

A beautiful smile came upon his face. I stood there in silence smiling back. Soon he dropped off to sleep. I told the family that I would return in a few hours.

At 10:00 a.m. I returned to the hospital and met the man's sister outside his room. She told me that while I was gone her brother had died, but that he had been able to sleep until 6:00 a.m. When he awoke, he knew he was about to die. Just before he passed away, he called his sister to his bed and told her he had a message for me.

"Tell the little lady I made it!" he said. His sister said that he kept repeating that phrase over and over again, "Tell the little lady I made it!" When he could no longer make a sound, his lips continued to move.

"I made it! I made it! Tell the lady I made it!"

10

HENRY

Wine is a mocker, strong drink is raging: and whosoever is deceived thereby is not wise.

Proverbs 20:1

After the church building was finished, I appointed Henry Herron to serve as superintendent of the Sunday School. Several members of his family warned me that he was unpredictable and unstable, but I stuck by my decision, thinking that the responsibility might be just what Henry needed to settle him down.

One day his sister Stella ran across the street to the parsonage and blurted out breathlessly, "Sister Sumrall, I hate to tell you this, but your Sunday School superintendent is standing down in front of Mr. Volgt's drugstore, drunk!" She told me that Henry's wife had gone after him, but he had refused to go home with her.

Mother and I got in the car, went by and picked up Henry's wife, and then drove to Volgt's drugstore. Sure enough, there stood Henry holding on to a light post.

I jumped out of the car, opened the back door and said, "Henry, get in the car." With his eyes blurring, he looked up. Again I said, "Get in the car!" He made an effort, but he was so drunk his wife and I had to assist him.

I knew nothing at all about alcohol, but I had heard somewhere that black coffee and tomato juice would sober up a drunk, so I poured both of them down Henry. It wasn't long before he became nauseated and lost the coffee, the tomato juice and—I suppose—the alcohol as well. For a while it looked as though he was going to lose his insides along with them.

When he was sober, Henry said, "I'm so ashamed. Will I have to apologize to the church?"

I told him, "This is a small town and

by now everyone knows what has happened. If you feel you owe the church an apology, that is up to you. If you want me to, I'll apologize for you."

I don't remember whether he apologized to the church or not. But one thing I do recall is that for as long as Mother and I served as pastors of that church Henry Herron never got drunk again, but instead lived a victorious life for Jesus.

11

THE JANITOR

...thou hast hid these things from the wise and prudent, and hast revealed them unto babes...

Luke 10:21

Our janitor, Mack, had a mental deficiency. None of his family were religious, so he came to church alone, never missing a service. He loved the little church and spent many happy hours there. He was a self-appointed janitor. We had no air-conditioning, so he came to church early to raise the windows to make the building more comfortable. He would dust the seats, piano, and pulpit. He stayed late after services to lower the windows, gather all the song books from

the pews and stack them neatly near the
front. He picked up all paper and trash
that had been dropped by careless per-
sons. To Mack the little church was a
very hallowed place. It was a joy to him.
Whenever we had an altar call, he always
came forward to pray.

One Wednesday night while kneeling
at the altar, suddenly "In Jesus' name"
echoed from the opposite side of the
church. Then I heard a loud thud. I
walked over to the west side of the church
and lying on the floor was a six-foot, two
hundred pound man. He looked as
though he might be dead. The man on the
floor was an uneducated, but sincere
Christian.

Looking around, I asked what happened. Near the unconscious man was
Mack. Walking slowly toward me, he
pointed to the man on the floor and said,
"He was praying and kept asking God to
let him feel His power. Over and over he
would say, 'Lord, I want to feel Your
power. Please knock me out. Oh, God, I
beg You in Jesus' name, knock me out.' I
kept watching him and he was crying so
hard...I told God He had better knock
him out. If you don't, I will." He went

on to say, "I just wanted to help. Since God didn't answer, I doubled up my fist and said, 'In Jesus' name,' and hit him as hard as I could."

I thought the man would never regain consciousness. When he did, he did not realize what had happened. He rubbed his head and said, "I don't think I should ask God to knock me out again. He has quite a whollop!"

I do not know if the man ever knew who knocked him out.

12

GEORGE

Not by works of righteousness which we have done, but according to his mercy he saved us...

Titus 3:5

One day I saw a pickup truck stop in our driveway. A man got out and came to the door. He introduced himself as George and handed me several bags of groceries. He said that he butchered meat for several stores in town.

"I'm not a Christian," he told me. "But I like what you and your mother are doing. I can't come to church but once a week and that will be on Sunday night."

Later his wife told me that George gambled every Saturday night until the early hours of Sunday morning. He would come home, sleep most of the day on Sunday, and then come to the church in the evening. Each Monday morning he brought bags of groceries to our place, opened his billfold, and gave us several dollars.

George lived near the highway and raised chickens. Occasionally a chicken would wander onto the road and be struck by a car and killed. Whenever that happened, George would call one of his boys by name and tell him, "We aren't paying the preachers enough. Catch two chickens and take them to the parsonage." We could always tell when a car had killed one or more of George's chickens because we could hear his boys coming two blocks away. They would swing the chickens overhead and toss them up and down until they made all kinds of noises.

I always told the boys how much we appreciated the chickens. They were shy so they would run home as fast as they could.

One Sunday afternoon there came a terrible storm. Only two men came to church that night. One of them was George. I knew that both men were sinners. We gave them an entire service. We sang hymns, took prayer requests, and prayed. After we had taken the offering, I opened my Bible and gave those two men a forty-five-minute sermon from Revelation 21:7,8: *He that overcometh shall inherit all things; and I will be his God, and he shall be my son. But the fearful, and unbelieving, and the abominable, and murderers, and whoremongers, and sorcerers, and idolaters, and all liars, shall have their part in the lake which burneth with fire and brimstone: which is the second death.*

The two men sat almost like statues. I gave an altar call, then the dismissal prayer. I heard later that the men said I preached a good sermon. They knew I was preaching it to them; they had to, because no one else was there. They said that from then on they were going to peek in and see if there was anyone else in the church before they went in.

Several years after Mother and I had left Ferriday to go into the evangelistic field, I had occasion to pass through Ferriday on my way to a meeting in another city. I hadn't planned to stop, but I needed to fill up the car with gas.

It so happened that while I was there Mr. Calhoun pulled into the same station to fill up. He recognized me and said, "You must go see George. He is not expected to live and has never become a Christian." So while my car was being serviced, Mr. Calhoun and I drove down to George's home in his car.

As we walked up to George's room, a nurse was just coming out. "How is George?" I asked. She shook her head, indicating that it was just a matter of time.

As I stood by George's bed I could see that he had suffered a severe stroke and had no way of expressing himself. He had lost control of his whole right side, his face was drawn, and his voice was completely gone. It was obvious that he was not long for this world. I took his left hand which still had feeling in it and said, "George, if you know who I am, squeeze my hand." He squeezed my hand!

I continued, "If you want to become a Christian, squeeze my hand." And he did.

When I finished praying, I looked around the room. Everyone was on their knees, weeping.

I said, "George, if you feel that God has saved you and you are ready for heaven, squeeze my hand one more time."

I thought he was never going to turn loose of my hand!

When I left, everyone in the room was still crying.

A few days later, George passed away.

13

THE STRANGER

But my God shall supply all your need according to his riches in glory by Christ Jesus.

Philippians 4:19

Being a newcomer to Louisiana, I was surprised when I received an invitation to speak for a youth rally. When I looked in my clothes closet, I did not have one appropriate dress to wear. I had no money and the church people were not able to help. Our income was small. We would receive as little as thirteen cents one week, and on another we might get as much as three dollars! Mother and I made it a matter of prayer concerning my going to the rally.

The following Wednesday night a new man attended the prayer meeting. After everyone was gone, he said to Mother, "God told me to bring you some money." He reached in his pocket and gave me a handful of money. Then he reached in a different pocket and handed Mother several bills. It seemed he had money in ALL his pockets.

We wondered where he got so much money. Mother's hands were full and so were mine. When he pulled out the last roll of bills, I sat down. My hands could hold no more, so I put it in my lap. I asked him if he was sure he wanted to give us all that money. He said, "I have plenty more where this came from."

When he left, both of us were dumbfounded! It was our first time to see him and we never saw him again. When we returned home we put our treasure in a large fruit bowl. I have no idea the exact amount he gave us, but it was several hundred dollars, which was a lot of money to us. I have often wondered where the man came from and where he went. Could it have been my guardian angel?

I spoke at the rally in my new dress!

14

GOD IS NOT MOCKED

Be not deceived; God is not mocked: for whatsoever a man soweth, that shall he also reap.

Galatians 6:7

One morning at seven o'clock a lady came and asked us to pray for her husband to get a job.

While she was there a man came to the door and gave us a ten pound bag of sweet potatoes. When I brought them in the lady began to cry saying she had no food in her house for her children. This touched my heart so I gave her the potatoes.

Several days after this no one brought us any food. We began to pray and ask the Lord why the people had stopped helping us.

That day a man came to visit us and said he felt led to bring some food, but several people told him that we had so much food that we were giving it away. I was shocked and asked who had told him that. He said, "A lady told my wife you were giving bags of food away and you gave her a ten pound bag of sweet potatoes."

I did not deny or agree that I gave the potatoes away. But I had been to see a businessman asking him if he would help the father of this family get a job. He said as a favor to me he would try. In less than two weeks the businessman contacted this family saying that Miss Sumrall had asked him to give her husband a job and he could now come to work. This made the lady feel condemned. She came to my house and apologized, saying God spoke to her that the axe is laid at the root of the tree and if she didn't stop trying to hurt me and Mother Sumrall, God would cut her off.

It wasn't long until I heard that she was attacking us again. I prayed that God would speak to her.

Again she came to the parsonage to apologize. I put my arms around her and said I forgave her. Her face was pale and her lips were trembling as she said, "But you don't understand; God spoke to me that if I continued to attack you and Mother Sumrall, He would cause my bowels to gush out like Judas'. God said that I could not destroy His children with my lies."

In spite of this, she was soon attacking us again. Because she attended our church, I did not tell the people in our congregation about her criticizing us.

One day a man rushed up on this lady's porch. He said, "Come, one of your sons has been hit by a car!" They arrived at the scene of the accident before the ambulance. A sheet had been spread over the boy's body. She rushed over, lifted the sheet and saw that her son was dead. She cried out, "Oh, God! My bowels are gushed out like Judas'."

She told me that when the coroner examined her son there was not a bruise on any part of his body except his stomach was bursted open and his bowels had run out on the pavement. As this lady told me this story, she wept bitterly.

15

GOD'S FAITHFULNESS

But seek ye first the kingdom of God, and his righteousness; and all these things shall be added unto you.

Matthew 6:33

Since we had no car when we first arrived in Ferriday, Mother and I walked everywhere we went. During those first few weeks and months I walked so much I began to have problems with my feet. Then a strange thing happened. By the end of the day, my feet and stockings would be bloody, yet there would be no open sores anywhere on my feet. I told a doctor about it, that the blood seemed to be coming from the pores of my skin.

The doctor examined my feet and

agreed that that was probably what was happening. He said that sometimes when one part of the body, like the feet, is subjected to severe stress and punishment over a period of time, it goes into "agony" and bleeds through the pores. He said that in all his years of medical practice he had known only one other person who had bled through the pores, a man who lifted heavy objects all day long.

Later on, Lester returned from overseas and visited the church and parsonage for the first time. While he was there, he saw me take off my shoes and noticed that my stockings were bloody. He felt bad and said to me, "I have very little money, but I'm going to buy you a car."

He had agreed to speak at a rally in Shreveport, Louisiana, about 185 miles northwest of Ferriday, so he and I took the bus and went on to the meeting early. When we got there, we went out looking for a car. We found a little blue Ford which Lester purchased for us.

The following day Lester was on his way to Dallas, Texas, to preach in another meeting and I set out for Ferriday in my little blue Ford. Three young ladies asked me if they could ride with me as far as

Monroe, Louisiana, about a hundred miles away. Several times en route the girls wanted to stop for soda pop and candy. I would agree but would never buy anything for myself because I needed what little money I had for gas, which was selling then for about thirteen or fourteen cents a gallon. I was surprised that the young ladies did not offer to buy a single gallon of gas, nor did they offer to buy me a cold drink or a candy bar.

When we reached Monroe, I turned off the highway and let the girls out. The gas gauge began to register empty, so I stopped and bought 75¢ worth of gas, which left me a grand total of 25¢ to my name! Still pretty far from home, and all alone, I wasn't the least bit anxious or afraid. It never occurred to me to worry about having a flat tire or car trouble on that lonely stretch of road. I was so happy as I drove down the highway, I lifted my voice in song and praise to the Lord for my new car!

I drove for miles and did not see a single house, neither did I pass one car. All I could see were bayous on either side of the road. I arrived home just before dark and blew the horn as I drove up in front of the parsonage. Mother came outside and both of us rejoiced that God had given her a good son and me a good brother to provide us with transportation.

Although in many ways those were some of the most difficult days of our lives, I will always remember Ferriday with joy and gratitude to God for His wonderful call and marvelous provision.

1. Mother Sumrall, 2. Leona Sumrall, 3. & 4. Jerry Lee Lewis' Parents, 5. Jimmy & Jerry's Grandfather,
6. Jimmy Swaggart, 7. Jerry Lee Lewis, 8. Jimmy & Jerry's Uncle Henry, 9. Jimmy's Father, 10. Uncle Lee